Sales Struggles?

Don Barnes

Published by Don Barnes, 2024.

About the Author

Don Barnes is the founder and author of Life Works in Threes!™ E-books. He is a lifelong Texan who has traveled extensively while taking a keen interest in human behavior. His curiosity about life and what drives humans led him to the discovery of how life works in threes. He coined this term as the *Tryune Concept*.

Don attended college on an athletic scholarship and then embarked on a 30-year career in the oil and gas industry. During his post O&G days, he got involved in a polar-bonding technology for lubrication and a liquid ozone technology used to replace chlorine for water treatment.

Along the way, he worked on his Tryune discovery, in hopes of someday sharing his findings with those struggling unnecessarily in life. What Don surmised from 40+ years of R&D was that people were struggling unnecessarily in life because they were not aware that "life works in threes." People, for the most part, are living their lives <u>by chance</u> rather than <u>by choice.</u>

From this, he began focusing on the "mechanics of life" which shows formulas for success with subjects such as *life, health, money, purpose and so forth*. When humans are able to grasp the Tryune Concept, they can apply the formula of topics that interest them and begin eliminating the struggle. This epiphany is what triggered his Tryune venture and is now on the path of sharing this amazing discovery with all who desire to improve on their lives.

Don currently resides in Southern California and Texas while overseeing his businesses and investments.

Life Works in Threes™

When I was a kid growing up, no one sat me down and said, "Okay Don, I'm going to show you how life works so that you can navigate your way through adulthood." I graduated from school, got married and went about my way with the "learn as you go" concept. It was kind of like putting together a backyard swing set without a set of instructions. Lots of frustration and do-overs, for sure!

My discovery of the "triune" word and noticing how things come together in threes is really what set me off on researching that maybe "life comes in three" ...sort of a mechanical approach to managing life, if you will. I combed the libraries and bookstores for information on this and found one book on the subject that was written back in 1951. The author's name was John S. Arant.

What Mr. Arant had to say is this "For lack of a better name, I have called this *The Triangle of Triumph* and therefore, consistent with the name, since most of these conclusions are built on the geometric figure of the triangle." He continued "All Life and all lives are seated in, and circumscribed by, the triangle. The Author and Source and Director of all life is Himself triune in character – Father, Son, and Holy Spirit. Man is of triple nature – body, mind, and spirit – and within those three there are many triangles – desires, development, decay; intellect, will, sensibilities. Of this "paced interlude in the midst of eternity" which we call time there is the triangle of Past, Present, and Future. Space – that limitless and measureless element of the physical universe – is best known in terms of Height, Breadth, and Depth. Try building yourself some triangles along the lines of your Will, your Work, your Way – You will find some interesting angles.

So, for the first time, I realized that life is designed in a mechanical way to come in threes. That means you don't have to rely on wishing and hoping things turn out okay. You can actually look at the three parts that a particular thing is made of and then apply them to get what you're wanting. Like a three-ingredient recipe or a combination lock. With a combination lock, you need the three exact numbers to unlock the lock...otherwise you will continue to struggle.

Some 40 years later, I accumulated things that work in threes and that's when I knew I needed to share this with anyone wanting answers. To have success/harmony in your life, just apply the three parts of an area you're working on, and things will fall into place. I also learned that the recipe for success with just about anything is by doing these three things, consistently – THINK positively, SPEAK positively and ACT positively. For example, if I want to be a successful artist. I would think to myself "I can do this because I have the talent." Then I would speak it this way "Yes, I am working on my art degree and plan to do portraits professionally." Finally, I would act on that by taking art classes and continue crafting my skill. Eventually, I will see the positive results/success I'm looking for.

Conversely, if I think positively but speak negatively...it will cancel out. Or if I speak positively but have no positive action going on...nothing will happen.

I looked up "How Life Works" and "The Mechanics of Life" and these are really talking about the biology of how our cells work and other chemistry. TRYUNE WORKS! teaches that life is kind of like building blocks. Pick a topic you may be struggling with. See the three parts that topic consists of and then start applying them...on a consistent basis. That will help you overcome the struggle and get you back in harmony/success with how life works.

For 30+ years I was a golf instructor (by accident). My two kids had some success playing junior golf and so friends and neighbors would ask me to show them and their kids how to play golf successfully. From all of this, I got pretty good at watching golfers on the driving range and could spot right away why they were struggling with hitting bad golf shots. I was able to do that because I knew the three steps to hitting good golf shots. I learned them from studying golf and played for several decades. I "broke the code" for me so to speak.

So now you know that life works in threes. You can live your life *by choice* rather than *by chance* and that my friend... is the key to a fulfilling life.

Introduction

You might be surprised that there are a fair number of sale types and all of them require training to obtain a certain skill level for success. The other point I'd like to make is that "sales" is a forever-thing from the CEO all the way to the receptionist. Why? Because sales are a "transference of feelings." When customers see how everyone in an organization is upbeat and positive about their company and products/services…that eventually translates to sales.

I personally spent 40+ years in Outside sales for oil and gas markets. My sales log showed over 35,000 sales calls and 700,000+ miles of driving time during my career. So, I can relate, first-hand, the challenges and skills necessary to have success. Been there and done that!

Sales in business can vary widely based on factors like the nature of the product or service, the target market, and the sales approach. Here are some common types of sales in business:

1. **Direct Sales**: This involves selling directly to customers, either in-person, over the phone, or through online channels. Direct sales often involve a salesperson engaging with potential customers to persuade them to make a purchase.
2. **Indirect Sales**: Indirect sales involve selling through intermediaries, such as wholesalers, distributors, or retailers. The product or service passes through these intermediaries before reaching the end customer.
3. **Retail Sales**: Retail sales involve selling products directly to consumers through physical or online retail stores. Retail sales can include both in-store and e-commerce transactions.
4. **B2B Sales (Business-to-Business)**: B2B sales involve selling products or services from one business to another. This type of sales often involves longer sales cycles, relationship-building, and customized solutions to meet the needs of other

businesses.

5. **B2C Sales (Business-to-Consumer)**: B2C sales involve selling products or services directly to consumers. This can include selling through retail stores, e-commerce websites, direct mail, or other channels.

6. **Inside Sales**: Inside sales involve selling remotely, typically over the phone, email, or online chat. Inside sales reps often work from a central location rather than traveling to meet with clients in person.

7. **Outside Sales**: Outside sales involve selling in-person, often by traveling to meet with clients or prospects. Outside sales reps may visit clients at their offices, attend trade shows, or conduct product demonstrations on-site.

8. **Consultative Sales**: Consultative sales involve taking a consultative approach to selling, where the salesperson acts as a trusted advisor to the customer. This involves understanding the customer's needs and offering personalized solutions rather than simply pushing products or services.

9. **Transactional Sales**: Transactional sales involve quick, one-time sales transactions with customers who have a clear need for the product or service and are ready to buy. These sales typically involve lower-priced items and require less relationship-building.

10. **Solution Sales**: Solution sales involve selling comprehensive solutions to customers' problems rather than just products or services. This often requires a deep understanding of the customer's business challenges and the ability to tailor a solution to meet their specific needs.

11. **Technical Sales**: Technical sales involve providing engineering solutions to engineering issues. This requires the technical salesperson to explain in technical terms how a technical issue can be resolved.

Now you know of the types of sales that businesses engage in, and many businesses may use a combination of these approaches depending on their industry, target market, and sales goals.

My discovery of the Tryune Concept

Before we dive into sales struggles and how to overcome them, let me share my discovery of the Tryune Concept and how life works in threes. It all began in the summer of 1982.

I grew up with parents who treated everyone with decency and respect. My three older sisters and I were raised in a home that was "middle-class traditional." We lived in modest homes in different small towns, attended school and church on a regular basis and celebrated all the traditional holidays. Eventually we settled during the spring of 1964 in the big city of Houston, Texas. I'll never forget the vastness of the city and hearing sirens from police cars, fire trucks and ambulances on a regular basis. I was excited and scared at the same time.

Once settled in this fast-paced city, I finished my growing-up years with an academic diploma and sweetheart intact. I got a job, bought a car, got married, bought a house and produced two beautiful babies in a span of about 5 years. Talk about having to grow up fast!

Things went from great in my childhood to absolute misery in my young adulthood. I began to struggle with my job because deep down I just hated what I was doing. This problem created a snowball effect because soon after, my weight, my finances, my relationships, my happiness and everything else worth saving was going down the drain. I eventually hit a level of frustration that I had never experienced before and didn't know how to get out of it. My cry for help was for anyone or anything to come to my rescue. I just ran out of solutions for my situation.

This is when my discovery happened.

One night shortly after my meltdown, while sleeping soundly, the word "triune" began to softly pound in my head like a mantra. I woke up a little startled and decided to go look up the word in my favorite dictionary (this was WAY before Google.) The definition said '**triune** (try-une) – 1) a group of three things; united. 2) Being 3 in 1 such as *humans are mental, physical and spiritual.* I scratched my head, got a glass of water and went back to bed.

The next day while driving around town, I began thinking about things that I was taught in my younger years that came in threes. My Boy Scout manual taught that to have **character**, I needed to be *1) physically strong, 2) mentally awake and 3) morally straight.* My high school football coach would say emphatically "If you want to be **a good football player**, you have to be *1) mobile 2) agile and 3) hostile!*" My first sales manager shared with me that to be **a successful salesman**, I needed to have *1) sales skills, 2) product knowledge and 3) a good image.*

"Hmm", I thought, "wonder if there are other examples out there of things that work in threes?" So, some 40 years later, I have researched and discovered that many, many things work in threes. What this message was telling me is that to achieve success or balance in any significant area of my life, the three things that area consisted of had to be present, continuously. That's when I had my epiphany. This discovery was telling me the secret to how life <u>really</u> works...in a mechanical way.

Tryune is a play on the word "triune" as an invitation to "try" this concept. Furthermore, we do not say that life <u>only</u> works in threes. Life also works in ones, twos, fours and so on. What has been observed though is that the many things significant to life, just so happen to come and work in threes. That's what is being shared in this book.

Now, you are about to see 40+ years of research and proof that life works in threes. I did not make up any of these topics. I invite you to research them on the internet to validate what is written here. There are some interesting facts that most of us have never realized...until now.

How Life Works in Threes (around 200 examples)

<u>LIFE</u>

Humans consist of *body, mind and soul.*

A human's basic needs are *health, income and provisions.*

A human's basic wants are *comfort, gain and approval.*

Our minds are made up of the *conscious, the subconscious and the unconscious.*

Philosophy explains *the id, the ego and superego.*

Atoms consist of *protons, neutrons and electrons.*

Motion is explained by *three basic laws.*

Science falls under three main branches: *natural, social and formal sciences*

Time is *past, present and future...*at the same time.

Electricity consists of *ohms, amperes and voltage.*

Music's basic elements are *duration, pitch and timbre.*

Democracy is a government *of the people, by the people and for the people.*

U.S. branches of government are *the judicial, the executive and the legislative.*

Armed Forces protect us on *land, air and sea.*

Environmentally, we are asked *to reduce, recycle and re-use.*

The news program gives us *the news, sports and conditions.*

Our days consist of *morning, afternoon and evening.*

Three months in each season of the year

Our main meals are known as *breakfast, lunch and dinner.*

A balanced diet consists of *good proteins, carbohydrates and fats.*

Traditional Family consists of *father, mother, and child(ren)*

<u>SCIENCES</u>

Three major branches of natural science – *(physical, earth/ space and life sciences)*

Three major branches of modern physics - *(classical, relativistic, quantum)*

Three major branches of biology *(botany, zoology, microbiology)*

Three spatial dimensions: *height* (up/down), *width* (left/ right) and *depth* (forwards/backwards)

Three-gauge bosons (photon, gluon, W&Z bosons)

Three types of elementary particles *(leptons, quarks, gauge bosons)*

Three quarks in every proton *(two "up" and one "down")*

Three primary colors of light *(red, green, blue)*

Three color tone properties *(hue, value, chroma)*

Three laws of motion (*Newton's laws*)

Three laws of planetary motion (*Kepler's laws*)

Three layers of the Sun's interior (*core, radiative zone, convective zone*)

Three layers of the Sun's atmosphere (*photosphere, chromosphere, corona*)

Three types of meteorites (*iron, stony iron, stony*)

Three types of galaxy shapes (*elliptical, spiral, irregular*)

Three substances of the universe (*normal matter, 'dark matter', 'dark energy'*)

Three phases of the moon (*new moon, first quarter, full moon*)

Three planetary regions (*temperate, sub-tropical, tropical*)

Three layers of the Earth (*crust, mantle, core*)

Three components of an ecosystem (*producers, consumers, decomposers*)

Three types of rocks (*igneous, sedimentary, metamorphic*)

Three types of fossil fuels (*coal, crude oil, natural gas*)

Three hydrological processes (*evaporation, condensation, precipitation*)

Three basic types of (meteorological) precipitation (*liquid, freezing, frozen*)

Three types of substances *(mono-constituent, multi-constituent, UVCB)*

Three phases of (normal) matter *(solid, liquid, gas)*

Three types of covalent chemical bonds *(single, double and triple bonds)*

Three isotopes of hydrogen *(protium, deuterium, tritium)*

Three atoms in each molecule of water *(two hydrogen atoms and an oxygen atom)*

Three endings to salts *(-ide, -ite, -ate)*

Three requirements for fire *(fuel, oxygen, heat)*

Three nucleotide bases in a genetic codon

Three domains of life *(archaea, bacteria and eukaryotes)*

Three major groups of flowering plants *(monocots, eudicots, magnolids)*

Three major functions that are basic to plant growth and development: *(photosynthesis* [making sugars], *respiration* [metabolizing those sugars], and *transpiration* [water vapor loss]

Three things that the chlorophyll in plants needs for photosynthesis to take place: *(sunlight, carbon dioxide and water)*

Transpiration serves three roles: *(cooling the plant, moving minerals* and *sugars through the plant,* and *maintaining the turgidity pressure* [stiffness] *of the plant's cells)*

Three parts of an insect's body *(head, thorax, abdomen)*

<u>BIOLOGY</u>

Three types of cones in the retina, relating to the three primary colors

Three semi-circular canals in the ear *(lateral, anterior, posterior)*

Three sections in the ear *(outer, middle, inner)*

Three ossicles in the middle ear *(malleus, incus, stapes)*

Three segments to each limb *(proximal, mid, distal)*

Three bones in each arm *(humerus, radius, ulna)*

Three joints in the arm *(shoulder, elbow, wrist)*

Three joints in the leg *(hip, knee, ankle)*

Three joints in the elbow *(humeroulnar, humeroradial, proximal radioulnar)*

Three functional compartments in the knee joint *(the femoropatellar, medial femorotibial* and *lateral femorotibial articulations)*

Three types of fibrous joints *(sutures, gomphoses, syndesmoses)*

Three types of bone in each hand (*carpals, metacarpals, phalanges*)

Three types of bone in each foot (*tarsals, metatarsals, phalanges*)

Three bones (phalanges) in each finger and in each toe (*proximal, intermediate, distal*)

Three layers of skin (*dermis, epidermis, hypodermis*)

Three components of a cell (*cell membrane, nucleus, cytoplasm*)

Three types of blood vessels (*arteries, veins, capillaries*)

Three types of blood cells [*red* (erythrocytes), *white* (leukocytes), *platelets* (thrombocytes)]

Three processes of the intestinal tract (*ingestion, digestion, excretion*)

Three germ layers (*Endoderm, Mesoderm, Ectoderm*)

Three parts of a human tooth (*crown, neck, root*)

Three organs of otolaryngology (*ear, nose, throat*)

Three major body systems (*digestive, circulatory, respiratory*)

Three parts to a neuron: (*soma* [*cell body*], *axon, dendrites*)

Three main parts of the brain (*forebrain, midbrain, hindbrain*)

Three parts of the forebrain (*cerebrum, thalamus, hypothalamus*)

Three parts of the midbrain (*colliculi, tegmentum, cerebral peduncles*)

Three parts of the hindbrain (*cerebellum, pons, medulla*)

Three membranes enclosing the brain (*dura mater, arachnoid, pia mater*)

The brain operates on three levels: *consciously* (for cognitive thought and declarative memory); *subconsciously* (for pre-planned actions and procedural memory); and *unconsciously* (for breathing, heart beating, etc.)

Our conscious mind is fed from three sources: *our senses* (which can be fooled); *our memory* (which is flawed); and *our imagination* (which is inventive)

Three aspects of the human mind (*memory, intellect, will*)

Three parts of the human personality (*id, ego, superego*)

The sum of human capacity consists of three abilities (*thought, word and deed*)

Three times of man (*birth, life, death*)

Three periods of the Gait Cycle (*initial double limb support, single limb support, and terminal double limb support*)

<u>MUSIC</u>

Three types of musical notes (*sharps, flats, naturals*)

Three aspects of a song (*lyrics, melody, rhythm*)

Three types of musical chords (*root, third, fifth*)

MATHEMATICS

Three types of a real number (*positive, negative, zero*)

Three parts to any arithmetic operation: for addition: *augend, addend and sum* - for subtraction: *minuend, subtrahend and difference* - for multiplication: *multiplicand, multiplier and product* - for division: *dividend, divisor and quotient*

Three laws of arithmetic operations (*commutative, associative, distributive*)

Three types of equivalence relation (*reflexivity, symmetry, transitivity*)

Three types of symmetry operations (*translation, rotation, reflection*)

Three geometries (*Euclidean, spherical, hyperbolic*)

The number 3 is the basis of an entire branch of mathematics, called trigonometry (from the Greek *trigonon* "triangle" + *metron* "measure")

Three trigonometric functions (*sine, cosine, tangent*)

Three types of average (*mean, mode, median*)

GRAMMAR

Three logical operators (*AND, OR and NOT*)

Three laws of logic (*identity, noncontradiction, excluded middle*)

Three parts of a logical syllogism (*major premise, minor premise, conclusion*)

Three grammatical parts to a sentence (*subject, verb, complement*)

Three persons in grammar [*1st person* (I/we), *2nd* (you or your), *3rd* (he/she/it/they)]

Three genders in grammar [*masculine* (he/him), *feminine* (she/her), *neuter* (it)]

Three forms of comparison in grammar [*positive, comparative* (more, -er), *superlative* (most, -est)]

Three cases in (English) grammar [*subjective/nominative* (he), *objective/accusative* (him) and *possessive/genitive* (his)]

Three parts of a narrative (*beginning, middle, end*)

Components of an essay (*introduction, body, conclusion*)

Elements of a rhetorical appeal (*ethos, pathos, logos*)

Aspects of a story (*plot, characters, setting*)

<u>RELIGION</u>

The Creator – *omniscient, omnipotent, omnipresent*

Christian God – *Father, Son, Holy Spirit*

Jesus – *The Way, The Truth, The Life*

Ancient Near East- *Qudshu, Astarte, Anat*

Classical Antiquity – Many dieties came in threes

Hinduism – Para Brahman is *Brahma, Visnu, Shiva*

Ancient Celtic Cultures – *many example of triad dieties*

Buddhism – *The three jewels*

Taoism – *The three pure ones*

Islam – *Fear, Hope and Love*

Baha'i - *Intention, Power and Action*

Confucianism – *Benevolence, Wisdom and Courage*

<u>OTHER TRIUNE EXAMPLES</u>

3 Coins in a Fountain

3 Days of the Condor

3 Miles in a League

3 Goals in a Hat Trick

3 Piece Suit

3 Feet in a Yard

3 Books in Lord of the Rings

3 Ring Circus

3 Ships of Christopher Columbus

3 Sheets to the Wind

3 Books in a Trilogy

3 Wheels on a Tricycle

3 Wise Men

3-Legged Race

3 Ring Circus

3-Wheeler

3 Cornered Hat

3 Dimensional

3 Musketeers

3 R's (reading, 'riting, 'rithmatic)

3 Sides of a triangle

3 Races in the Triple Crown (horse racing)

3 Angles in a Triangle

3 Trimesters in a Pregnancy

3 Flavors in Neapolitan Ice Cream

3 Stars in Orion's belt

3 Barleycorns in an Inch

3 Hands on a Clock (with the Seconds Hand)

3 Colors in a Flag

3 Minute Egg

3 Great Pyramids at Giza

3 Holes in a Bowling Ball

3 Colors in a Set of Traffic Lights

3 Minutes in a Boxing Round

3 Teaspoons in a Tablespoon

3 Legs on a Stool

3 Monastic Vows (Obience, Stability, Conversatio Morum)

3 Body Types: Endomorph, Mesomorph, Ectomorph

3 Ring Notebooks

3 Germ layers: Endoderm, Mesoderm, Ectoderm

3 Species of Homo: Homo habilis, Homo erectus, Homo sapiens

3 Basic parts of a camera: Lens, Shutter, Sensor

3 Stages of a Project lifecycle: initiation, planning, execution

The Truth, The Whole Truth and Nothing but the Truth

Life, Liberty and the Pursuit of Happiness

Hear no Evil, See no Evil, Speak no Evil

National motto of France/Haiti: Liberty, Equality, Fraternity

Paper, Rock, Scissors

Ready, Aim, Fire

On Your mark, Get Set, Go

Olympic medals of gold, silver, bronze

Types of joints (ball & socket, hinge, pivot)

Stages of a rocket launch (launch, orbit, re-entry)

Parts of a joke (setup, delivery, punchline)

Primary components of a transistor (emitter, base, collector)

Primary components of an airplane (fuselage, wings, empennage)

Basic components of a computer: CPU, memory, storage

Three phases in the development of technology (*eotechnic* [*mechanical*], *paleotechnic* [*steam-powered*] and *neotechnic* [*electric-powered*]

Communication systems require three components (*transmitter, channel, receiver*)

The list goes on. See if you can find more examples as they are everywhere in our universe. Now that you know that life works in threes (with proof!), we can begin to apply this concept to whatever topics we want.

So, to overcome struggles in sales, we need to apply the three areas that sales consist of – YOU, YOUR SKILLS and YOUR MARKET. Let's get started!

YOU
SALES
YOUR
SKILLS
YOUR
MARKET

SALES

Choosing sales as a profession can be an exhilarating journey filled with dynamic challenges and rewarding successes. It's like stepping onto a bustling marketplace where every interaction holds the promise of forging valuable connections and sealing deals. One of the most enticing aspects of sales is its versatility—it's not just about pushing products but also about building relationships, understanding customer needs, and finding innovative solutions to their problems. If you're someone who thrives on human interaction and loves the thrill of negotiation, then sales might just be your calling.

Beyond the thrill of the chase, a career in sales offers ample opportunities for personal and professional growth. Each sales encounter is a chance to learn something new, whether it's about your product, your industry, or the art of persuasion itself. Success in sales isn't just about hitting quotas; it's about continuously honing your communication skills, mastering the art of persuasion, and developing a keen business acumen. The skills you acquire in sales—like *resilience, adaptability, and empathy*—are invaluable not only in your professional life but also in your personal endeavors.

Moreover, sales is a field that rewards initiative and drive. Unlike some professions where your advancement might be limited by factors beyond your control, in sales, your success is often directly proportional to your effort. Whether you're working for a multinational corporation or starting your own entrepreneurial venture, the potential for growth and financial reward in sales is virtually limitless.

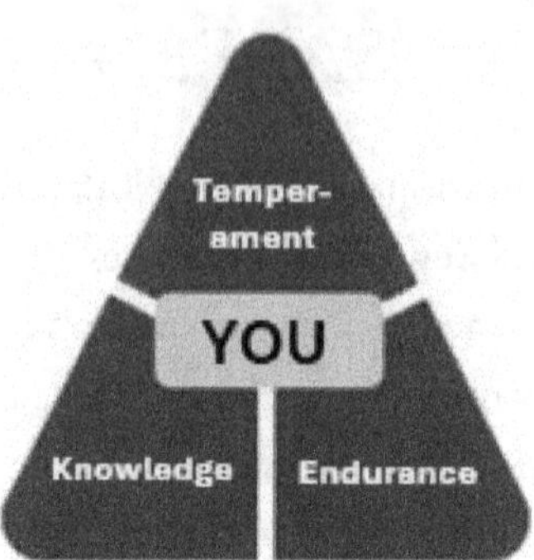
Temper-
ament
YOU
Knowledge
Endurance

YOU

Understanding what it takes to be a successful salesperson is like unlocking the secrets to a well-guarded treasure chest—it requires a blend of *skill, mindset, and a sprinkle of charisma*. Firstly, successful salespeople possess **excellent communication skills**. They're adept at listening attentively to their clients, understanding their needs, and articulating how their product or service can fulfill those needs. Communication isn't just about talking; it's about building rapport, asking the right questions, and truly empathizing with the customer's perspective.

Secondly, **resilience** is the secret sauce that keeps successful salespeople going, even in the face of rejection or setbacks. Rejection is a natural part of the sales process, but what sets top performers apart is their ability to bounce back stronger than ever. They view rejection not as a personal failure but as an opportunity to learn and improve. A positive mindset, coupled with resilience, allows successful salespeople to persevere through tough times and emerge victorious in the end.

Lastly, successful salespeople are **masters of time management and organization**. They understand the value of their time and prioritize tasks that directly contribute to their sales goals. Whether it's prospecting for new leads, following up with existing clients, or preparing persuasive presentations, they know how to allocate their time effectively to maximize productivity. Additionally, they're proactive in seeking out opportunities rather than waiting for them to come knocking. By staying organized and proactive, successful salespeople ensure that they're always one step ahead of the game.

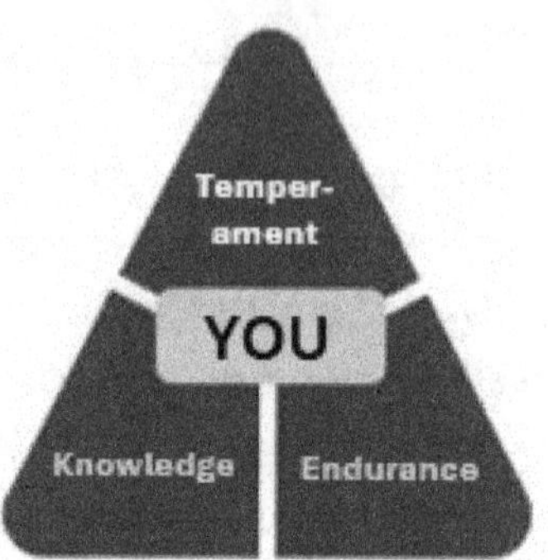
Temper-
am·ent
YOU
Knowledge
Endurance

Temperament

In the vibrant world of sales, having the right temperament is like having a trusty compass guiding you through uncharted waters. First and foremost, a **friendly and approachable demeanor** is key. Successful sales professionals understand the importance of building genuine connections with their clients. Whether it's a warm smile, a friendly greeting, or a sincere interest in the client's needs, being genuinely likable goes a long way in winning trust and fostering long-term relationships.

Flexibility is another essential trait for sales professionals. The sales landscape is ever-changing, with new trends, technologies, and customer preferences constantly emerging. Those who thrive in this environment are adaptable and open-minded, willing to embrace change and adjust their strategies accordingly. Whether it's learning about a new product feature or pivoting their approach to accommodate a client's unique requirements, flexibility allows sales professionals to stay ahead of the curve and remain competitive in the fast-paced world of sales.

Lastly, determinationis the backbone of a successful sales temperament. Rejection and setbacks are par for the course in sales, but it's how you bounce back from them that truly matters. Determined sales professionals view challenges as opportunities for growth and refuse to let setbacks deter them from their goals. They maintain a positive attitude even in the face of adversity, using each setback as a steppingstone to propel them closer to success. With a *friendly disposition, adaptability, and determination* as their guiding stars, sales professionals navigate the twists and turns of the sales journey with confidence and grace.

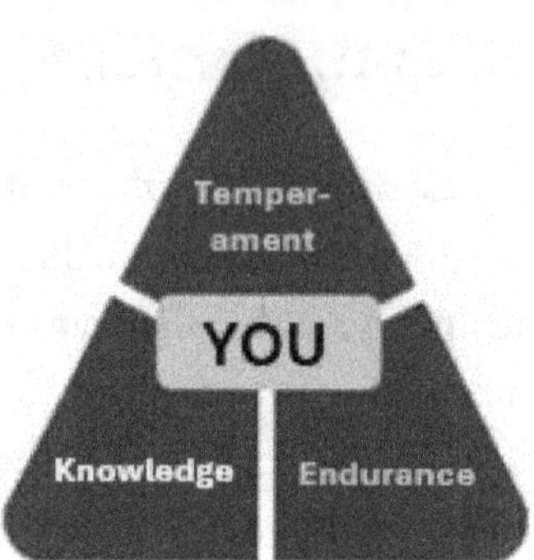
Temper-
ament
YOU
Knowledge
Endurance

Knowledge

Picture this: you're at a bustling marketplace, surrounded by curious customers eager to learn about what you have to offer. In this lively scene, **knowledge is your greatest asset.** Understanding your products and services inside out is like wielding a powerful tool that allows you to showcase their value with confidence and conviction. When you're well-versed in what you're selling, you become a trusted advisor rather than just a salesperson. Customers appreciate authenticity, and having in-depth knowledge demonstrates your commitment to providing them with the best possible solution to their needs.

Moreover, **knowledge breeds credibility.** Imagine you're in a conversation with a potential client, and they ask you a question about a specific feature of your product. Without skipping a beat, you're able to provide them with a detailed explanation, instilling trust and confidence in your expertise. When customers feel confident in your knowledge, they're more likely to trust your recommendations and ultimately make a purchase. In today's competitive market, credibility is currency, and having a deep understanding of your products and services is the golden ticket to earning it.

But the importance of product knowledge goes beyond just making sales—it's about **building lasting relationships**. When you take the time to truly understand your products and services, you're better equipped to anticipate and meet your customers' needs. By providing personalized recommendations and solutions, you show that you value their business and are committed to helping them succeed. In the end, it's these meaningful connections that lay the foundation for long-term loyalty and success. So, whether you're selling widgets or wares, remember that knowledge is your greatest ally in the journey to sales success.

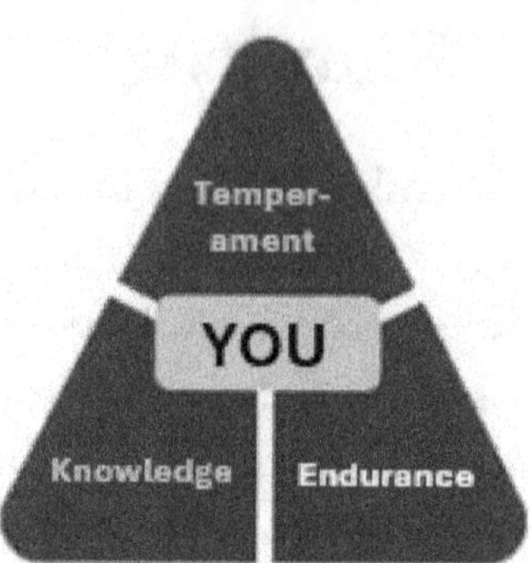
Temper-
ament
YOU
Knowledge
Endurance

Endurance

Welcome to the exhilarating world of sales, where the journey to success is more like a marathon than a sprint. In this dynamic arena, patience, endurance, and strategic pacing are your trusted companions on the road to victory. While some may view sales as a mad dash to the finish line, seasoned professionals know that sustainable success is achieved through consistent effort and steady progress over time. Just like training for a marathon, mastering the art of sales requires dedication, perseverance, and a long-term perspective.

In the fast-paced world of sales, it's easy to get caught up in the frenzy of short-term wins and immediate gratification. However, those who approach sales with a marathon mindset understand the value of playing the long game. Rather than focusing solely on closing deals here and now, they prioritize building lasting relationships and nurturing leads over time. Just as a marathon runner conserves their energy and paces themselves for the long haul, successful sales professionals invest time and effort into cultivating trust and rapport with their clients, knowing that the rewards will be sweeter in the end.

Moreover, like running a marathon, sales requires careful planning, strategy, and resilience in the face of challenges. Just as a runner prepares for obstacles along the racecourse, sales professionals anticipate objections, competition, and market fluctuations. They understand that setbacks are inevitable, but it's how they respond to adversity that sets them apart. With determination and grit, they push through the tough moments, staying focused on their goals and maintaining momentum even when the going gets tough. So, whether you're lacing up your running shoes or sharpening your sales pitch, remember that success is a journey, not a sprint, and embracing the marathon mindset is the key to reaching the finish line.

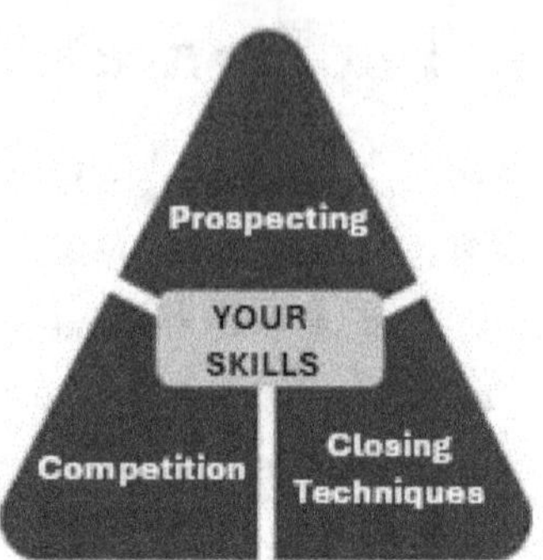
Prospecting
YOUR
SKILLS
Competition
Closing
Techniques

YOUR SKILLS

Sales is like a finely choreographed dance, where mastering the right moves can lead to a standing ovation from your audience. Firstly, **active listening** is your backstage pass to understanding your customers' needs. Rather than just waiting for your turn to speak, truly listening to your clients allows you to uncover valuable insights and tailor your pitch to address their specific pain points. By showing genuine interest in their concerns and asking thoughtful questions, you demonstrate that you're not just there to sell but to provide solutions that genuinely meet their needs.

Next up on the stage is **the art of persuasion.** Think of it as weaving a compelling story that captivates your audience and leaves them eagerly reaching for their wallets. Persuasive sales professionals understand the power of storytelling, using anecdotes, case studies, and testimonials to illustrate the value of their products or services. By painting a vivid picture of the benefits your offering brings, you create an emotional connection that resonates with your clients and motivates them to take action. Whether it's highlighting the time-saving features of your software or showcasing the transformative results of your consulting services, mastering the art of persuasion is key to winning hearts and closing deals.

Last but certainly not least is the **ability to build rapport and trust**. Just like a friendship, successful sales relationships are built on a foundation of trust, respect, and mutual understanding. Whether you're meeting a client for the first time or nurturing a long-term partnership, building rapport is essential for creating a positive connection and fostering loyalty. By being genuine, reliable, and transparent in your interactions, you demonstrate that you're not just in it for the sale but for the long haul. So, dust off your dancing shoes, hone your listening skills, perfect your storytelling, and get ready to woo your audience with your irresistible charm and undeniable expertise.

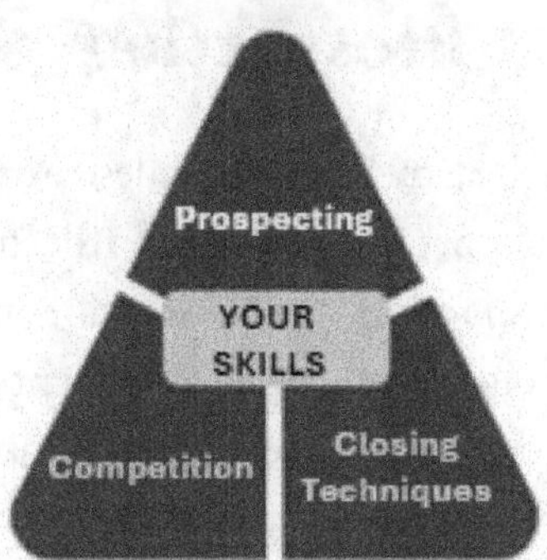

Prospecting
YOUR
SKILLS
Competition
Closing
Techniques

Prospecting

Ah, prospecting—the heartbeat of the sales profession! Imagine it as sowing the seeds of opportunity in the fertile fields of your market. **Without diligent prospecting**, your sales pipeline resembles a barren desert rather than a flourishing garden of potential. It's not just about finding leads; it's about nurturing relationships and uncovering hidden gems that could blossom into lucrative deals. In the dynamic world of sales, prospecting is your compass, guiding you towards new horizons and untapped opportunities.

Moreover, effective prospecting lays the groundwork for sustainable success. Think of it as casting a wide net to reel in the big fish. By **continuously expanding your pool of prospects,** you create a steady stream of opportunities that fuel your sales efforts. Whether it's networking at industry events, leveraging social media channels, or cold-calling potential clients, the key is to cast your net far and wide, always on the lookout for new leads to add to your pipeline. After all, in the game of sales, it's not just about who you know but also who you're yet to meet.

Furthermore, prospecting is about more than just quantity—**it's about quality.** Not all leads are created equal, and effective prospecting involves identifying those with the greatest potential for conversion. By conducting thorough research and qualifying your leads based on criteria such as budget, authority, need, and timeline (BANT), you ensure that you're investing your time and resources wisely. By focusing your efforts on high-quality prospects, you maximize your chances of success and avoid wasting precious resources on dead-end leads. So, grab your prospecting pickaxe and get ready to unearth a treasure trove of opportunities waiting to be discovered!

The best thing you can do for your prospecting efforts is to ask for referrals. Get in the habit of asking a satisfied customer if they anyone who could use your products/service and watch your business grow!

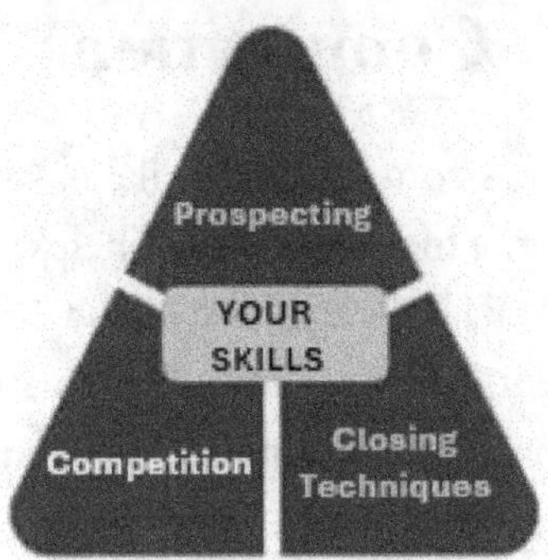
Prospecting
YOUR
SKILLS
Competition
Closing
Techniques

Competition

Understanding your sales competition is like having a map in a treasure hunt—it guides you to the hidden gems and helps you navigate the twists and turns of the market landscape. Just like a friendly game of chess, knowing your opponents' moves allows you to strategize and stay one step ahead. **By studying your competition**, you gain valuable insights into their strengths, weaknesses, and market positioning. This knowledge arms you with the tools to differentiate yourself and highlight your unique value proposition, giving you a competitive edge in the crowded marketplace.

Moreover, understanding your sales competition fosters a culture of continuous improvement and innovation. **Rather than viewing competitors as adversaries**, see them as sources of inspiration and motivation. Analyze their strategies, product offerings, and customer feedback to identify areas where you can outshine them. By keeping a close eye on the competition, you can adapt and evolve your own approach to stay relevant and meet the ever-changing needs of your customers. After all, in the dynamic world of sales, standing still is not an option—continuous learning and innovation are the keys to staying ahead of the curve.

Furthermore, understanding your sales competition **allows you to anticipate and preempt their moves**, turning potential threats into opportunities. By staying informed about industry trends, market shifts, and emerging competitors, you can proactively address challenges and capitalize on new openings. Whether it's adjusting your pricing strategy, enhancing your product features, or refining your messaging, the insights gained from understanding your competition empower you to make informed decisions that drive growth and success. So, embrace the spirit of friendly competition, and let it fuel your quest for sales excellence!

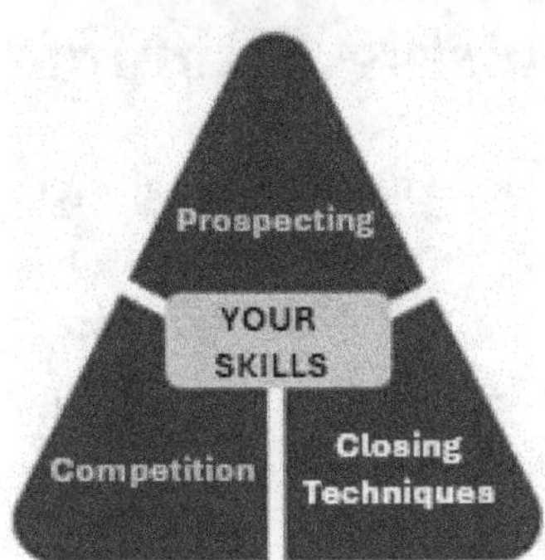
Prospecting
YOUR
SKILLS
Competition
Closing
Techniques

Closing Techniques

Closing the deal is the grand finale of the sales journey, like the satisfying ending to a captivating story. Mastering effective closing techniques is like having a magic wand that transforms potential into profit. Firstly, **the assumptive close** is like extending a friendly hand to lead your customer across the finish line. By assuming the sale is already made and presenting the next steps with confidence, you gently nudge your customer towards saying yes. Whether it's asking for their preferred payment method or discussing delivery options, the assumptive close subtly guides the conversation towards finalizing the deal without applying undue pressure.

Next up is the **trial close**, a playful dance that tests the waters before taking the plunge. By gauging your customer's readiness to commit through subtle questions or trial offers, you create opportunities for them to express their interest and address any lingering concerns. Whether it's asking if they prefer the blue or red model or offering a free trial period, the trial close allows you to gather valuable feedback and overcome objections before making the final ask. It's like dipping your toe in the water before diving in headfirst, ensuring a smooth and seamless transition to the closing stage.

Last but certainly not least is the **partnership close**, a bold move that confidently seals the deal. By suggesting that we work together to collaborate on solutions for a project, you create a sense of urgency and momentum that propels them towards making a decision. By asking the customer what he/she thinks needs to be done, the partnership close inspires action and leaves little room for hesitation. Talking in terms of "we" versus "you", the customer lets down their guard and opens up with information needed to close a sale. So, whether you're gently guiding your customer towards the finish line or boldly leading the charge, mastering these closing techniques is the key to unlocking success in sales.

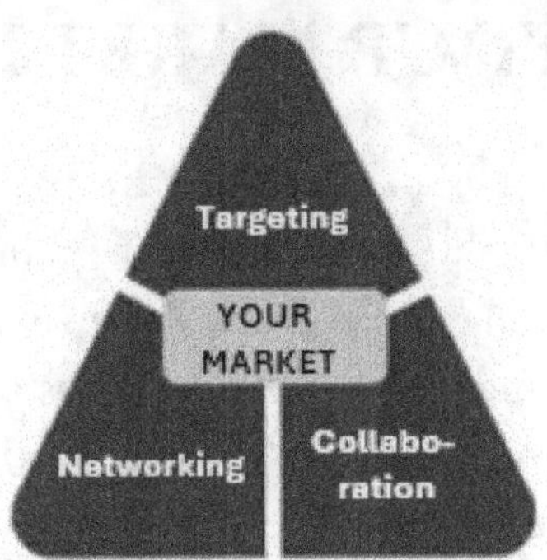
Targeting
YOUR
MARKET
Networking
Collabo-
ration

YOUR MARKET

Knowing your market is like having a treasure map that leads you straight to the pot of gold at the end of the rainbow! Understanding your market is like peering into a crystal ball, giving you valuable insights into the wants, needs, and preferences of your customers. By delving deep into your market's demographics, psychographics, and buying behavior, you gain a clear understanding of who your customers are and what makes them tick. Armed with this knowledge, you can tailor your sales approach to resonate with your target audience, creating personalized experiences that leave a lasting impression.

Additionally, knowing your market is like having a secret weapon in your arsenal. It allows you to identify untapped opportunities and capitalize on emerging trends **before your competitors even catch wind of them**. By staying ahead of the curve, you position yourself as a trusted advisor and industry leader, earning the loyalty and respect of your customers. Whether it's launching a new product line, entering a new market segment, or targeting a niche audience, understanding your market empowers you to make informed decisions that drive growth and success.

Finally, knowing your market fosters a culture of innovation and creativity. Rather than relying on guesswork or gut instinct, **you can leverage data-driven insights** to inform your sales strategies and tactics. By monitoring market trends, tracking customer feedback, and conducting regular market research, you stay attuned to the ever-changing needs and preferences of your audience. This allows you to adapt and evolve your approach in real-time, ensuring that you remain relevant and competitive in today's fast-paced business landscape. So, whether you're a seasoned sales veteran or just starting out, never underestimate the importance of knowing your market—it's the compass that guides you on your journey to sales success!

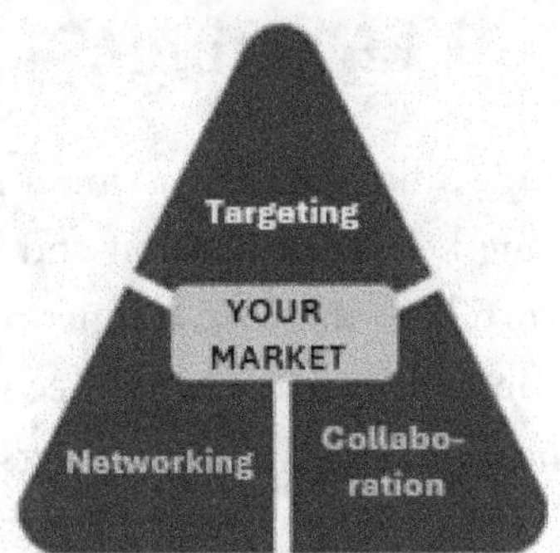
Targeting
YOUR
MARKET
Networking
Collabo-
ration

Targeting

When it comes to sales, deciding between a rifle approach and a shotgun approach is like choosing between precision and volume. Picture this: **the rifle approach** is like taking aim with a sniper rifle, carefully selecting your target and honing in on it with laser-like precision. By focusing your efforts on a specific niche or high-value prospects, you maximize your chances of success and minimize wasted resources. It's all about quality over quantity, investing your time and energy where it matters most and hitting the bullseye every time.

On the other hand, **the shotgun approach** is like casting a wide net in the hopes of catching as many fish as possible. Rather than zeroing in on a single target, you spread your efforts across a broad spectrum of prospects, hoping that sheer volume will yield results. While this approach may seem scattergun at first glance, it can be effective in certain situations, such as when you're exploring new markets or generating leads for a diverse range of products or services. It's like sowing seeds in a field—some may fall on rocky ground, but others will take root and flourish, leading to a bountiful harvest in the end.

Ultimately, the choice between a rifle approach and a shotgun approach depends on your specific goals, resources, and target market. While the rifle approach offers precision and focus, the shotgun approach offers breadth and versatility. By understanding the strengths and limitations of each approach, you can tailor your sales strategy to suit your unique needs and maximize your chances of success. Whether you're taking careful aim with your sniper rifle or casting your net far and wide with your trusty shotgun, remember that success in sales is not just about hitting the target—**it's about finding the right balance between precision and volume.**

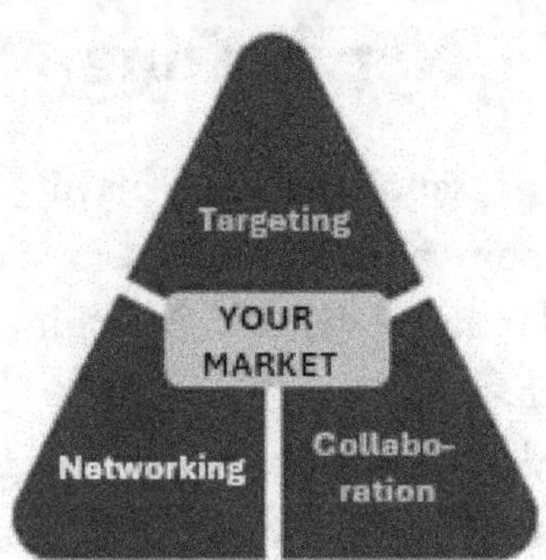
Targeting
YOUR
MARKET
Networking
Collabo-
ration

Networking

Networking—the secret sauce that adds flavor to the recipe of sales success! In the vibrant world of sales, building and nurturing relationships is like planting seeds that grow into fruitful partnerships. Networking is more than just swapping business cards at a conference or connecting on LinkedIn; **it's about forging genuine connections with people who can open doors**, offer insights, and champion your cause. Whether you're mingling at industry events, attending networking meetups, or engaging with prospects on social media, every interaction is an opportunity to expand your network and sow the seeds of future success.

Moreover, networking is like a treasure hunt where every new contact is a potential goldmine of opportunities. **By cultivating a strong network of contacts**, you gain access to valuable resources, insider knowledge, and referral opportunities that can give you a competitive edge in the market. Whether it's a warm introduction to a key decision-maker, a heads-up about an upcoming opportunity, or a word-of-mouth recommendation from a satisfied client, the benefits of networking extend far beyond just making new friends. It's like having a secret weapon in your arsenal that helps you navigate the twists and turns of the sales journey with confidence and ease.

Finally, networking is like a garden that requires care and attention to flourish. Building meaningful relationships takes time, effort, and genuine interest in the well-being of others. By investing in your network and offering value in return, **you create a virtuous cycle of reciprocity where everyone benefits.** Whether it's sharing industry insights, offering a helping hand, or simply being a supportive sounding board, the bonds you forge through networking can become invaluable assets throughout your sales career. So, dust off your networking shoes, polish your elevator pitch, and get ready to sow the seeds of success in the fertile soil of the sales profession!

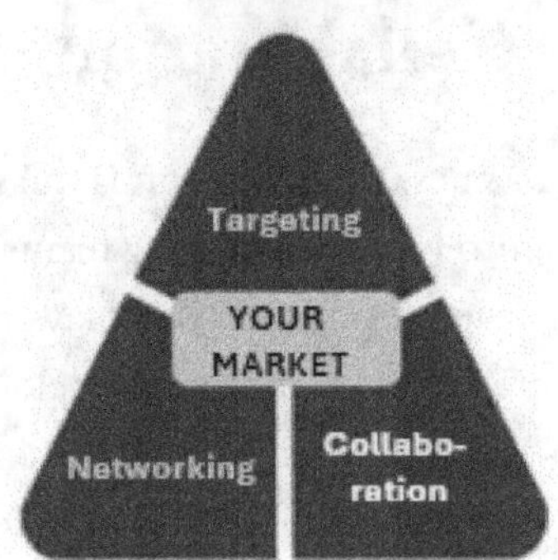

Targeting
YOUR MARKET
Networking
Collabo-
ration

Collaboration

In the dynamic world of sales, collaboration is the secret ingredient that transforms individuals into high-performing teams. Picture this: it's like a symphony orchestra where each member plays a unique instrument, coming together to create a harmonious melody. By collaborating effectively, **sales teams can leverage** the diverse skills, perspectives, and experiences of their members to achieve greater success than any individual could accomplish alone. Whether it's brainstorming new ideas, sharing best practices, or pooling resources to tackle a common challenge, collaboration fosters a spirit of camaraderie and unity that fuels innovation and drives results.

Moreover, **collaboration is like a relay race** where each team member plays a crucial role in passing the baton towards the finish line. By working together towards a common goal, sales teams can achieve greater efficiency, productivity, and effectiveness. Whether it's dividing tasks among team members, coordinating efforts across different departments, or aligning strategies to optimize outcomes, collaboration ensures that everyone is on the same page and moving in the same direction. It's like a well-oiled machine where each cog plays its part in keeping the wheels turning smoothly, ultimately propelling the team towards success.

Additionally, collaboration is not just about achieving short-term sales targets—it's about building lasting relationships and fostering a culture of trust and mutual support. By **collaborating with colleagues, clients, and partners**, sales professionals can create win-win scenarios that benefit everyone involved. Whether it's partnering with other businesses to offer joint promotions, collaborating with clients to co-create customized solutions, or teaming up with colleagues to share knowledge and expertise, collaboration opens doors to new opportunities and unlocks the full potential of teamwork. So, whether you're a seasoned sales veteran or a newcomer to the field, remember that collaboration is the key to unlocking greater success and achieving your goals with a friendly and collaborative spirit.

Temper-
ament
YOU
Knowledge
Endurance
SALES
Prospecting
YOUR
SKILLS
Competition
Closing
Techniques
Targeting
YOUR
MARKET
Networking
Collabo-
ration

SUMMARY

Sales, often underrated, is indeed a noble profession, akin to being a trusted guide leading others towards solutions that enhance their lives. Think of it as being a matchmaker, connecting people with products or services that fulfill their needs and aspirations. **Sales professionals are like the unsung heroes of commerce**, bridging the gap between supply and demand with integrity and expertise. Whether it's helping a family find their dream home, a business owner streamline their operations, or a student discover their passion, sales professionals play a vital role in shaping the world around us for the better.

Also, **sales is a profession built on relationships, empathy, and trust.** It's about understanding the hopes, fears, and dreams of your customers and guiding them towards solutions that align with their values and priorities. Sales professionals are like trusted advisors, offering insights, recommendations, and support every step of the way. Whether it's providing expert advice, offering a sympathetic ear, or going the extra mile to exceed expectations, the noblest sales professionals are driven not just by profits, but by a genuine desire to make a positive difference in the lives of others.

Finally, sales is a profession that rewards *hard work, perseverance, and integrity.* It's not just about closing deals; it's about building lasting relationships based on honesty, transparency, and mutual respect. Sales professionals who uphold these values earn the trust and loyalty of their clients, paving the way for long-term success and fulfillment. Whether it's navigating through challenging negotiations, overcoming objections with grace, or standing firm in the face of adversity, the noblest sales professionals approach their work with integrity and dignity, leaving a positive legacy that extends far beyond the bottom line. So, whether you're a seasoned sales veteran or just starting out, remember that sales is more than just a job—**it's a noble calling that empowers you** to make a meaningful difference in the world with a friendly and compassionate spirit.

Invitation

Whether you're a neophyte or seasoned veteran in sales, I invite you to go back over this book again and pick one or two areas you may want to improve on. There's no such thing as a perfect person or salesperson, so just relax and be yourself out there. Don't overwhelm yourself with TMI (too much information) in this book. **One or two tips at a time** should suffice.

I think it's important, based on my experience, to have a "servant" attitude when calling on prospects/customers. You know, doing "for" people rather than doing "to" people. The golden rule of treating others as we would like to be treated goes a long way to building credibility in your market. Remember, "it takes years to build credibility and one day to ruin it." **ALWAYS TELL THE TRUTH.**

I've also observed over the years that **three things need to be present to have a successful** sales career or even a year, for that matter. And that is this: 1) You need to have polished sales skills to have a chance at making sales. The more you practice...the better you'll get. 2) You need to sell a product/service that is credible. If you're good at selling but your product/service is inferior or a "me too" item, it will be hard to make a living. And 3) You need a market that is ripe. If you're the greatest salesperson in the world with excellent products/services...it won't matter if very few are buying.

Through all the years of being in sales, I never really thought of myself as a "salesman" trying to "sell" something to somebody. My approach was to be a "helper." I would usually start off with a question when with a customer by asking "So, Mr. Customer, what keeps you up at night? If I can provide you a solution to your particular problem, does that sound like something you might be interested in?" Simple question...powerful results.

When you're with someone who is sharing their struggles with you...just smile at him/her and give them one of these. He/she will ask "What is that?" Then simply reply "Life Works in Threes."

Other titles coming out:

- **Weight Struggles?**
- **Abundance Struggles?**
- **Parenting Struggles?**
- **Romance Struggles?**
- **Purpose Struggles?**
- **Happiness Struggles?**
- **Life Struggles?**
- **Speaker Struggles?**
- **Time Struggles?**
- **Network Struggles?**
- **Marriage Struggles?**
- **Divorce Struggles?**
- **Money Struggles?**
- **Career Struggles?**
- **Dating Struggles?**
- **Caretaker Struggles?**
- **Forgiveness Struggles?**
- **Grieving Struggles?**
- **Success Struggles?**
- **Golf Struggles?**
- **Workplace Struggles?**
- **Stress Struggles?**
- **Shame/Guilt Struggles?**
- **Addiction Struggles?**

Quotes about Sales

"If you are not taking care of your customer, your competitor will."
- Bob Hooey

"Don't sell features. Sell how your customers will benefit from using your products/services." - Don Barnes

"It's not about having the best product. It's about having the best story." - Seth Godin

"The best salespeople aren't salespeople at all. They're information brokers." - Harvey Mackay

"Sales are to businesses, like oxygen is to humans. Without it your business will suffocate and die." - unknown

Remember,

When you get right down to it,

Life is about making choices.

Every day, all day long, that's what we do.

- *We chose to get out of bed or not.*
- *We chose to clean up or not.*
- *We chose what to eat all day.*
- *We chose to exercise or not.*
- *We chose to go to work or not.*
- *We chose to do a good job or not.*
- *We chose to come home or not.*
- *We chose to watch TV or do something constructive.*
- *We chose to bed at a decent hour or not.*

And the next day…we start all over again.

What is the meaning of this? Get good at choosing.

Before you can get good at choosing though…you need to understand how life works in threes.

When someone is struggling with a particular area or two, chances are they are "out of balance" with how life works. How does life work? Life works in threes.

If you're interested in personal topics like life, health, money or business topics like sales, time management and public speaking...TRYUNE WORKS! can shed some light on creating success in those areas.

The definition of TRIUNE is a group of three things; united. Being three in one, such as - humans are *mental, physical* and *spiritual beings.* The word TRYUNE is a play of the word TRIUNE, encouraging all to try this concept and help eliminate struggling unnecessarily.

LifeWorksInThrees.com